OCT 11 1999

OCT 11 1999

Peter Panini's CHILDREN'S GUIDE TO THE HAWAIIAN ISLANDS

Written and Illustrated by Stacey Kaopuiki

HAWAIIAN ISLAND CONCEPTS

DEDICATION

This book is a gift from many hearts.
Through the time, efforts, encouragement
and aloha of many people, this book and
its characters have become a reality.

It is in this spirit and on behalf
of all these people that we dedicate
this book to the children of Hawai‘i.

Published by Hawaiian Island Concepts
P.O. Box 6280, Kahului, Maui, Hawaii 96732

Copyright Text and Illustrations © 1990
Hawaiian Island Concepts

First Printing: June, 1990
Second Printing: October, 1990

Book design by Wagstaff Graphic Design, Maui, Hawaii.

Library of Congress Catalogue Card Number: #90-81735

ISBN # 1-878498-01-0

Printed in Hong Kong.

Aloha, my name is Peter Panini and this is my dog, Punahele. We would like to tell you about the special place in which we live.

Hawai'i, the 50th State

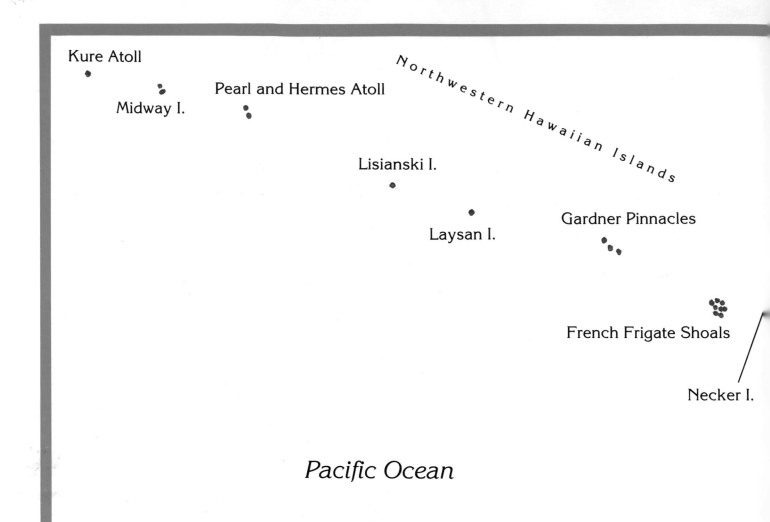

Kure Atoll

Midway I.

Pearl and Hermes Atoll

Northwestern Hawaiian Islands

Lisianski I.

Laysan I.

Gardner Pinnacles

French Frigate Shoals

Necker I.

Pacific Ocean

These are the Hawaiian Islands. They were formed millions of years ago by volcanos rising out of the sea.

There are 132 islands, atolls, reefs and shoals that stretch from Kure Atoll, 1523 miles across the Pacific Ocean, to the Big Island of Hawai'i.

The eight major islands are Ni'ihau, Kaua'i, O'ahu, Moloka'i, Lana'i, Kaho'olawe, Maui and the island of Hawai'i.

Each island has its own history and places of interest that make it different from the other islands.

Hawaiian Islands

State of Hawaiʻi

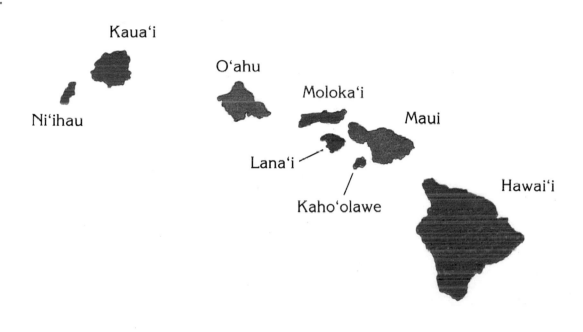

Nihoa I.

Kauaʻi

Niʻihau

Oʻahu

Molokaʻi

Lanaʻi

Maui

Kahoʻolawe

Hawaiʻi

Come on . . . Punahele and I would like to show you
some of these special places in the Hawaiian Islands.

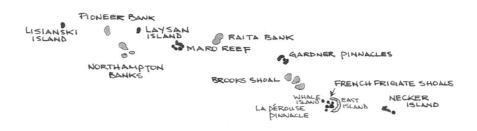

This group of tiny islands and atolls is called the Northwestern Hawaiian Islands and it is the home of the Hawaiian Islands National Wildlife Refuge.

No one lives on these islands except at small scientific and military camps on Kure Atoll and Midway Island.

Northwestern Hawaiian Islands

Although some of these islands are no more than specks in the ocean, they provide a safe and important home for many types of birds, fish, the green sea turtle, the Hawaiian monk seal and other marine mammals.

Hawaiian Island National Wildlife Refuge

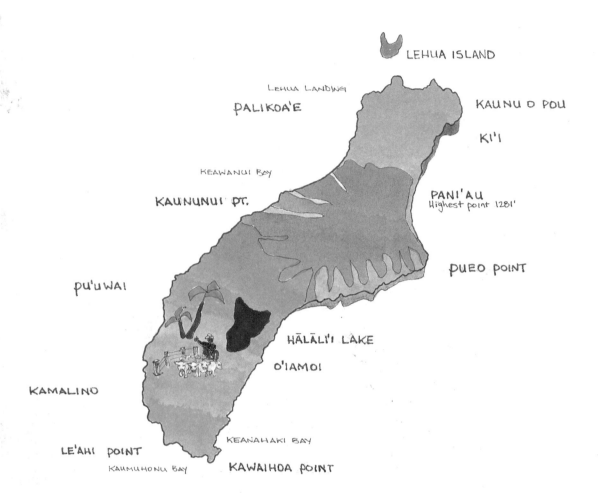

LEHUA ISLAND

LEHUA LANDING

PALIKOA'E

KAUNU O POU

KI'I

KEAWANUI BAY

KAUNUNUI PT.

PANI'AU
Highest point 1281'

PUEO POINT

PU'UWAI

HĀLĀLI'I LAKE

O'IAMOI

KAMALINO

KEANAHAKI BAY

LE'AHI POINT

KAUMUHONU BAY

KAWAIHOA POINT

NI'IHAU

This is the island of Ni'ihau. It is also known as the
"Forbidden Island" and is the seventh largest in size of the
Hawaiian Islands. The entire island has been privately
owned since it was bought from King Kamehameha V in
1863, and very few people are allowed to visit.

Along the shores of Niʻihau you can find a very tiny and delicate seashell that is found nowhere else in Hawaiʻi. It is called pūpū Niʻihau. After hundreds of these shells have been gathered, sorted and punched with holes, they are then strung into the beautiful and famous shell leis of Niʻihau.

Pūpū Niʻihau shell on the Island of Niʻihau

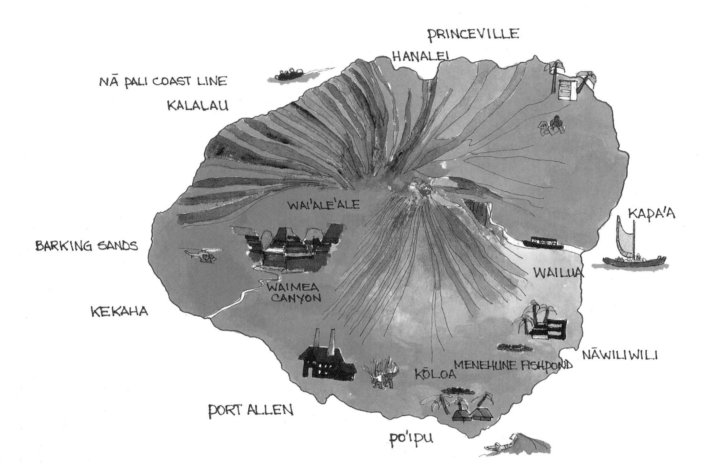

PRINCEVILLE
HANALEI

NĀ PALI COAST LINE
KALALAU

WAI'ALE'ALE

KAPA'A

BARKING SANDS

WAILUA

KEKAHA

WAIMEA
CANYON

MENEHUNE FISHPOND

NĀWILIWILI

KŌLOA

PORT ALLEN

PO'IPU

KAUA'I

Kaua'i is the fourth largest in size of the Hawaiian Islands and is also called the "Garden Isle."

Kaua'i is the oldest of the main Hawaiian Islands and is famous for its natural beauty. After millions of years of wind, rain and water, the works of these forces of nature can be seen on Kaua'i like nowhere else in Hawai'i.

Come on, we'll show you . . . .

Here, standing deep within a Hawaiian rain forest, you can visit the wettest spot on earth . . . .

Wai'ale'ale, Kaua'i

Or travel by helicopter to see the rich earth colors at
the spectacular "Grand Canyon of the Pacific."

Waimea Canyon State Park, Kaua'i

Take a lazy boat ride up the scenic Wailua River . . . .

Wailua River State Park, Kaua'i

Or visit the legendary Alakoko Fishpond. Hawaiian legends say that the *Menehune*, or the little people, built this fishpond in one night for a prince and princess that they loved. If you're lucky, you may even see a *Menehune*.

Alakoko Fishpond, Kaua'i

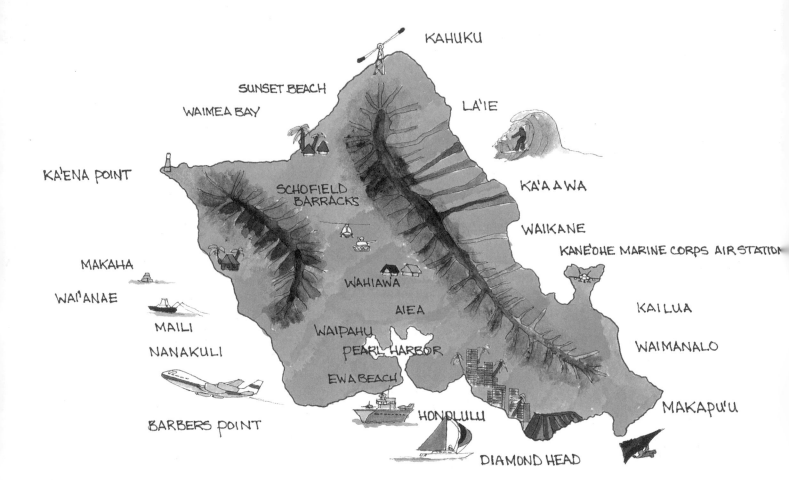

O'AHU

O'ahu, third largest in size of the Hawaiian Islands, is also known as the "Gathering Place." Most of the people of Hawai'i live and work on this island.

The city of Honolulu is an old and important harbor. Sailing ships from many different places once would stop to trade and take on new supplies and cargo before moving on. Come on. We'd like to show you some of the special places on O'ahu.

State Capitol Building

Downtown Honolulu

Market Place

Statue of King Kamehameha I and ʻIolani Palace

Honolulu is a city of over 838,500 people and is known as the business center of the Pacific.

Here you will find people from many different places doing business . . . in many different ways.

It is also a place where the kings and queens of Hawaiʻi once walked. From this palace, they governed the kingdom of Hawaiʻi.

Today, as in the past, Honolulu is the capital of the state of Hawaiʻi.

City of Honolulu, Oʻahu

On December 7, 1941, at 7:57 in the morning, Japanese warplanes bombed the naval base at Pearl Harbor. Many American servicemen were killed in the surprise attack.

It is silent now, but in the muddy waters you can still feel the events of that day that changed the course of history.

Arizona Memorial, Pearl Harbor, O'ahu

Enjoy the "Playground of the Pacific." Swim, surf and play in the shadow of Diamond Head, on the most famous beach in the world.

Waikiki Beach and Diamond Head, O'ahu

On "Family Sundays," the Bishop Museum presents music, dance, ethnic foods and many of the arts and crafts of old Hawai'i.

Inside the museum are displayed the ancient cloaks and helmets worn by the *ali'i,* or royalty; the weapons of the warriors; and many other treasures and artifacts from Hawai'i's past.

The Bishop Museum, O'ahu

The ocean has always been an important part of the lives of the people of Hawai'i.

There is no better place than Sealife Park to see and learn about the marine mammals, fishes and the ocean that surrounds us.

Sealife Park, O'ahu

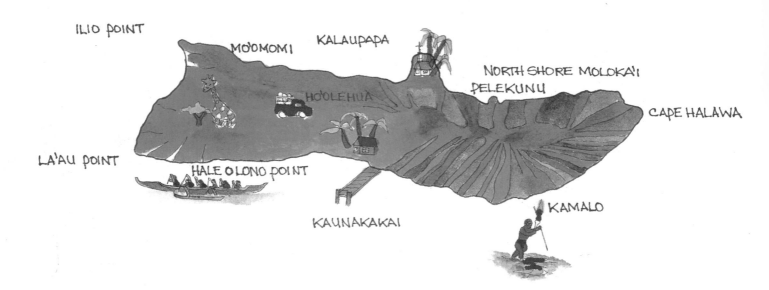

ILIO POINT

MO'OMOMI

KALAUPAPA

NORTH SHORE MOLOKA'I
PELEKUNU

HO'OLEHUA

CAPE HALAWA

LA'AU POINT

HALE O LONO POINT

KAMALO

KAUNAKAKAI

MOLOKA'I

This is the island of Moloka'i. It is the fifth largest of the
Hawaiian Islands and is best known for the warm aloha or
love of the people who live there. For this reason, Moloka'i
is also called the "Friendly Isle."

Long ago, people suffering from a disease called leprosy were sent to a faraway place called Kalaupapa. This was done to keep the disease from spreading to others.

Father Damien, a Catholic priest, is well known because he gave his life while helping and caring for the people of Kalaupapa.

By riding a mule down a steep and narrow trail across some of the highest sea cliffs in the world, you can visit Kalaupapa and Father Damien's church . . . .

Kalaupapa, Moloka'i

Or you can visit the wild animals that roam the drylands at the Moloka'i Wildlife Park.

Moloka'i Wildlife Park, Moloka'i

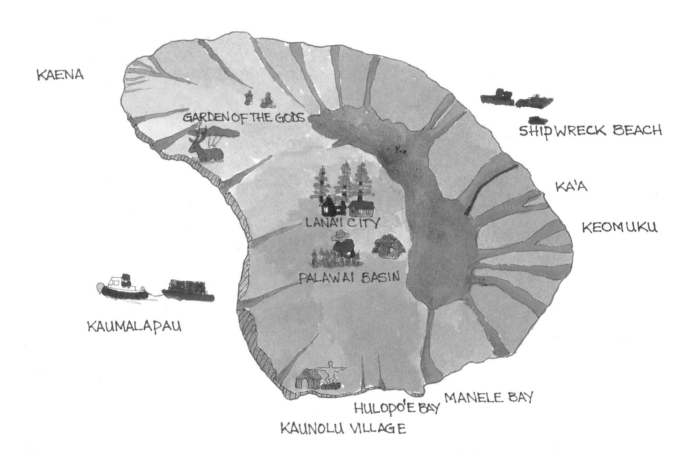

KAENA

GARDEN OF THE GODS

SHIPWRECK BEACH

KA'A

KEOMUKU

LANA'I CITY

PALAWAI BASIN

KAUMALAPAU

HULOPO'E BAY   MANELE BAY

KAUNOLU VILLAGE

LANA‘I

Known as the "Pineapple Island," and famous for its sweet pineapples, this is the island of Lana‘i. Sixth largest in size, Lana‘i is one of the largest pineapple plantations in the world.

Here you will see pineapple fields everywhere. The pineapples are picked when they start to turn yellow, loaded into bins and shipped to Oʻahu. There they are canned, made into juice or sent whole to stores all around the world.

Pineapple fields, Lanaʻi

By scratching on large boulders with sharp stones, ancient Hawaiians left mysterious drawings and symbols from the past.

Kahea, Luahiwa and Kaunolu Petroglyphs, Lana'i

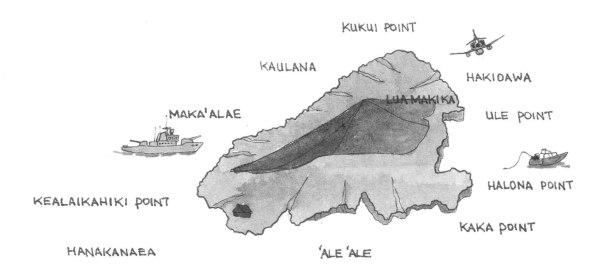

KUKUI POINT

KAULANA

MAKA'ALAE

LUA MAKIKA

HAKIOAWA

ULE POINT

KEALAIKAHIKI POINT

HALONA POINT

KAKA POINT

HANAKANAEA

'ALE 'ALE

KAHO'OLAWE

The smallest of the major Hawaiian Islands is
Kaho'olawe. Once a struggling cattle and sheep ranch, it
now stands barren and scarred from its use as a military
bombing range.

Although no one lives there now, there are Hawaiians
who are seeking to have the island returned to Hawai'i's
people.

Without using maps, the Hawaiians were able to travel far distances across the Pacific Ocean on their sailing canoes.

They relied on their knowledge of the sea, on the stars, the sun and certain points of land to guide them.

On Kahoʻolawe is a place called "Lae O Kealaikahiki," which means the point of the route to Tahiti.

It is said that the Hawaiians used this point to help guide them on their long voyage to Tahiti.

Lae O Kealaikahiki, Kahoʻolawe

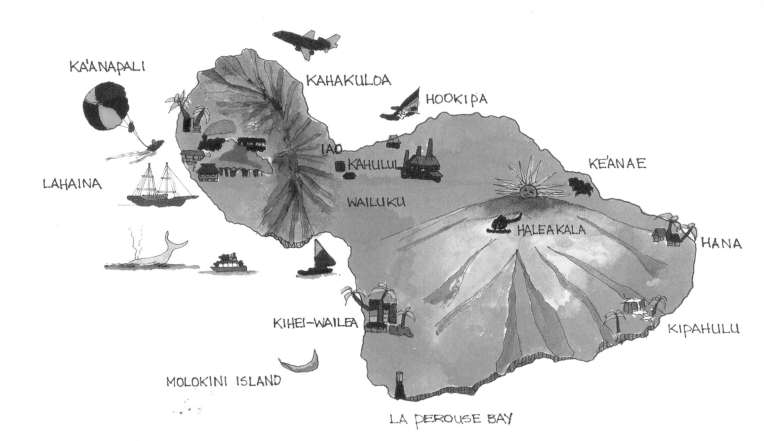

KA'ANAPALI

KAHAKULOA

HOOKIPA

IAO

KAHULUI

KE'ANAE

LAHAINA

WAILUKU

HALEAKALA

HANA

KIHEI-WAILEA

KIPAHULU

MOLOKINI ISLAND

LA PEROUSE BAY

MAUI

Maui, second largest of the Hawaiian Islands, is also called the "Valley Isle." Covered in green sugar cane fields, Maui is well known for its sandy beaches, windsurfing and the humpback whales who visit during the winter months.

Rising 10,023 feet above the sea, Haleakalā is a dormant volcano, or a volcano that is asleep. It has not erupted for a long, long time.

It was from Haleakalā, which means "House of the Sun," that the demigod Māui captured the sun and forced it to move more slowly across the Hawaiian skies.

Here you can see the rare silversword (‘āhinahina) plant and the state bird of Hawai‘i, the nēnē goose.

Haleakalā National Park, Maui

It is peaceful and quiet now, but this was once the site of a great battle of ancient Hawai'i between the warriors of King Kamehameha I and King Kahekili of Maui.

Legends say the fighting was so fierce that the streams turned red from the blood of wounded warriors.

Iao Valley State Park, Maui

King Kamehameha won this battle to control Maui and went on to unite the Hawaiian Islands.

On the windy north coastline of Maui, you can see the colorful and exciting sport of windsurfing.

People from many different countries come to windsurf at Hoʻokipa Beach, the windsurfing capital of the world.

Hoʻokipa, Maui

In the past, trains were an important part of the sugar plantations. Very few of the "sugar cane" trains are left.
This one will take you on a ride through the countryside from Lahaina to Ka'anapali.

Lahaina and Ka'anapali, Maui

Visit the historic whaling town of Lahaina.
Long ago, whaling ships often visited Lahaina while hunting whales. Today, rather than hunting whales, people come from all over the world to "whale watch" in the calm waters off Lahaina.

Lahaina, Maui

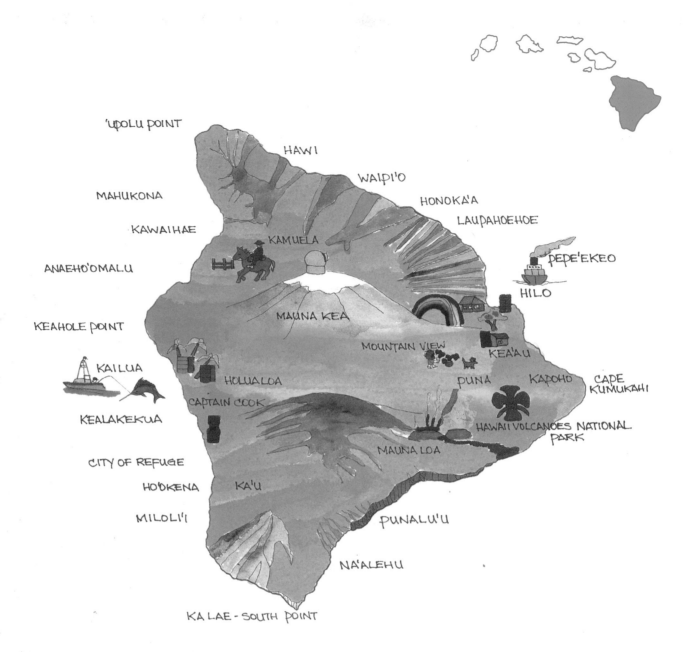

'UPOLU POINT
HAWI
WAIPI'O
MAHUKONA
HONOKA'A
LAUPAHOEHOE
KAWAIHAE
KAMUELA
PEPE'EKEO
ANAEHO'OMALU
HILO
KEAHOLE POINT
MAUNA KEA
MOUNTAIN VIEW
KEA'AU
KAILUA
HOLUALOA
PUNA
KAPOHO
CAPE KUMUKAHI
CAPTAIN COOK
KEALAKEKUA
HAWAII VOLCANOES NATIONAL PARK
CITY OF REFUGE
MAUNA LOA
HO'OKENA
KA'U
MILOLI'I
PUNALU'U
NA'ALEHU
KA LAE - SOUTH POINT

HAWAI'I

The Big Island of Hawai'i is the youngest and the largest of all the Hawaiian Islands. It is larger than all of the other islands combined. With the most active volcanos in the world still creating new land, the Big Island is continuing to grow in size.

Nicknamed the "Orchid Isle" because of the beautiful flowers grown there, it is also famous for its waterfalls, macadamia nuts, Kona coffee and rainbows.

Come on, we want to show you some of the exciting places here . . . .

The Hawaiian goddess of fire is called *Pele*. The legends say that *Pele* lives within the volcanos at Kilauea. When *Pele* is angry, she causes the volcanos to erupt and the lava to flow on its destructive journey to the sea.

Hawai'i Volcanoes National Park, Hawai'i

There are many places on the Big Island where you can sit quietly in a rain forest and watch the majestic beauty of a Hawaiian waterfall.

Akaka Falls State Park, Hawaiʻi

On the Kona side of the Big Island, the ocean is clear, deep and calm. It is here that fishermen from around the world come to test their skills trying to catch some of the biggest fish in the Pacific Ocean.

Kailua Kona, Hawai‘i

The two highest mountains in the State of Hawai'i are on the Big Island.

Here, atop snow-capped Mauna Kea, scientists from many nations have built the largest telescopes in the world. At night, they look deep into the dark, clear skies above Mauna Kea to learn more about our universe.

Mauna Kea 13,796 feet high

Astronomical Observatory of the University of Hawai'i   Mauna Loa 13,677 feet high

On the grassy slopes of Mauna Kea is the town of Kamuela. This is *paniolo,* or Hawaiian cowboy, country! It is also home of the Parker Ranch, the second largest privately owned cattle ranch in the United States.

Parker Ranch, Hawai'i

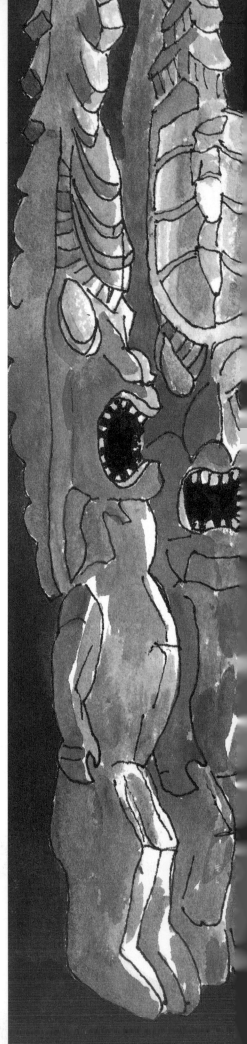

At Puʻuhonua O Hōnaunau, wooden gods silently stand watch over this city of refuge. In ancient Hawaiʻi, people in trouble would seek safety in places such as this. Here you would be protected from those who were trying to capture or punish you.

Puʻuhonua O Hōnaunau National Historical Park, Hawaiʻi

Well, it's been our pleasure to have shown you a few of our favorite places in Hawai'i. We hope that it has helped you to learn a little bit more about the special place that we live in.

But before we go, there's one more place we'd like to tell you about . . . .

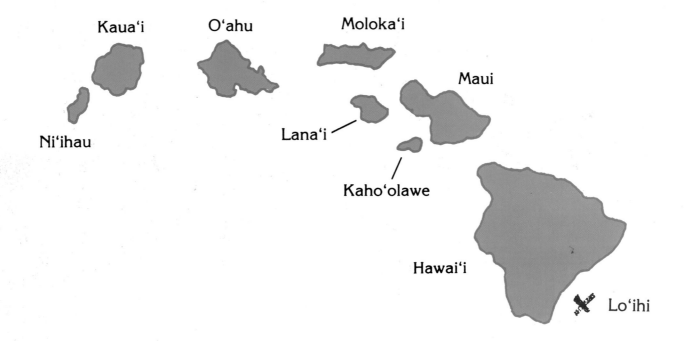

Kaua'i

O'ahu

Moloka'i

Maui

Ni'ihau

Lana'i

Kaho'olawe

Hawai'i

Lo'ihi

Not far from the Big Island of Hawai'i, deep beneath the ocean surface, something exciting is going on!

   An under-sea volcano, called Loʻihi, is erupting and a new island is being formed. This means that thousands of years from now, there will be a new Hawaiian Island, born from the sea . . . and another special place to visit!

ALOHA!

Loʻihi Seamount

GLOSSARY

ALI'I: Royalty; kings, queens, chiefs, princes, princesses.

ALOHA: Affection; love; also Hawaiian greeting for both "hello" and "goodbye."

ATOLL: A ring-shaped coral island surrounding a lagoon; in Hawaiian: *Mokupuni pālahalaha.*

DEMIGOD: Supernatural being possessing magical powers; in Hawaiian: *Kupua.*

'IOLANI: Royal hawk; a symbol of royalty because of its high flight in the heavens; also, the name of a palace and of a school in Honolulu.

LEPROSY: A mildly infectious disease due to a microorganism; in Hawaiian: *Ma'i Pākē.*

MĀKINI: A Hawaiian gourd mask; this is the helmet worn by Peter Panini and his dog Punahele.

MENEHUNE: Legendary race of small people who worked at night, building fish ponds, roads, temples; like Hawaiian elves.

NĒNĒ: Hawaiian goose.

PANIOLO: Common name for Hawaiian cowboy.

PELE: Hawaiian goddess of fire.

PETROGLYPHS: Drawings or carvings made in ancient Hawai'i that were scratched on rocks with sharp stones; a form of story-telling.

PŪPŪ NI'IHAU: A very tiny and delicate seashell found on the Island of Ni'ihau.